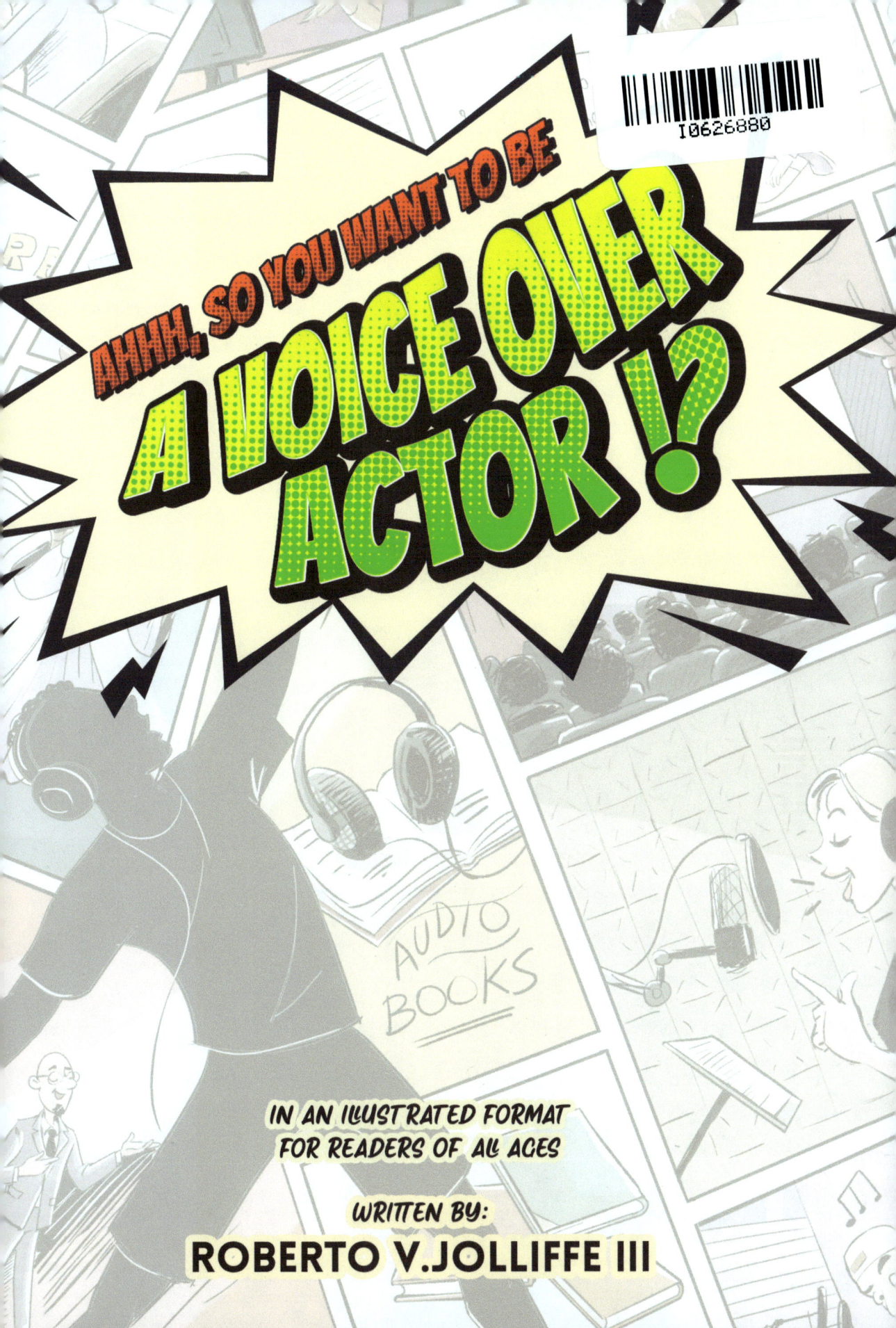

AHHH, SO YOU WANT TO BE
A VOICE OVER ACTOR !?

IN AN ILLUSTRATED FORMAT
FOR READERS OF ALL AGES

WRITTEN BY:
ROBERTO V.JOLLIFFE III

"I WOULD LIKE TO DEDICATE THIS TO MY FAMILY FOR ALWAYS SUPPORTING ME IN ANY ENDEAVOR I VENTURED INTO. I ALSO WOULD LIKE TO THANK MYSELF FOR ALWAYS BELIEVING IN ME EVEN WHEN THE PATH TO THE DESTINATION WASN'T ALWAYS CLEAR ON MY JOURNEY! TO MY KIDS JACEY, KHALI & BEAUX THE WORLD IS YOURS, GET AFTER IT."

- LOVE DAD -

CONTENT

Ever seen a commercial, movie trailer, or cartoon and thought, Wow, that is so cool! How can I do that!? Well, good thing you picked up this book! In this book, I will break down how you can become a voice over actor and how your unique voice can bring value to the industry.

I'm glad you're here. Want to know why? It's really simple, actually. With all the genres the voice over industry has to offer, your voice will always stand out amongst the 8 billion voices on this Earth. Want to know why? That is because it's YOURS. And trust me, somebody is going to like it!

First things, first, do not ever compare yourself to anyone else. After all, as the age-old adage goes, "Comparison is the thief of joy." Remember that everyone has their own talents, and that by failing to fully embrace your own voice, you may box yourself out of the right category for you.

Voice over acting gives you a chance to showcase your unique speaking style. Have an accent or your own quirky way of speaking? Or maybe you enjoy speaking in slang or a humorous manner?

If you answered yes to either question, rest assured that there are many opportunities for you to showcase your distinctive manner of speaking. For example, you could provide voice overs for spaces like local radio or television stations where your voice is native and authentic to the people of that region. Whether you're Hispanic, Black, White, from another country, or able to speak a dialect, there is a space for your voice to be heard and appreciated. In fact, I believe that it is imperative that you use your unique voice to show the industry (and the world) where you come from.

Did you know that you can use your unique voice to sell brands, products, provide information, or even to perform character acting?

What if I told you that you may have been working towards becoming a voice over actor since you were born? Take me for instance. I was a class clown in high school and a teacher once called on me to read passages where I, without even knowing it, was being tasked to voice over act. If I recall correctly the text featured Cowboys . . . or maybe it was Indians . . . or perhaps just some random character. I incorporated distinct voices for each character as I read. I did it to make it different from everyone's regular reading style. This came natural to me because growing up, I was always goofing around, mimicking commercials and things of that nature.

During college, I interned at a radio station, and I was also on the morning show. In this role, I would prepare for bits and set and record segments or drops. However, I never thought of what I was doing as voice over acting even though it incorporated aspects of utilizing my voice to act out scenes.

In my younger years, I didn't know there was an entire industry for voice over acting. I used to rap and produce songs, not fully realizing that I was gaining much needed skills, laying the foundation, and setting the course for my career in voice over acting.

The skills I learned throughout my life's journey were crucial to getting me where I am today in the voice over acting world.

Reflecting back on my past experiences, I realized that I had been working towards the field of voice over acting my whole life. Before I began taking acting and improv classes, I developed my skill set by playing and goofing off with those around me. I would mock or mimic people's voices, or just simply speak in a funny accent.

Chances are, you may already be working towards a career in voice over acting, especially if you love watching cartoons and commercials, or enjoy mimicking people's voices.

Taking a page out of my book, those random habits can be considered practice! When I first decided to get into voice over acting, I thought to myself, Oh, I already do this! I rap, I've made songs, interned on radio, done a little bit of this, and a little bit of that . . . The next question was, How do I translate all these skills to the voice over realm? Then, before I knew it, I had entered the world of voice over acting!

Now you can too!

EQUIPMENT

As with everything, you have to start somewhere. Don't be discouraged if you do not have access to top tier equipment. You don't need an in-home booth, a home studio, or even the top microphones, headphones or interfaces.

All you need is what you likely already have! In my case, I started off with a microphone and interface that cost $60 to $300, and the GarageBand computer application which was free on my MacBook!

My advice to you is to start where you are and with what you can afford. From there, put in the work to plant those seeds and before you know it, voilá, your fruits will be ready for harvesting!

Frankly, the hardest part about starting a career in voice over acting is beginning the process. You just need a basic microphone, headset, audio interface, and recording software. Also, purchasing acoustic foam wall padding, to minimize sound reflection, would also be beneficial. These acoustic foam pads are sold on online stores such as Amazon. You can use the foam to cover sections of a room to provide better sound quality and get as close to a reflectionless room as you can for your microphone.

I started off with a basic microphone which I placed on my desk. As I progressed in the field, I reinvested in my craft by improving the quality of my equipment. There are many tiers of recording equipment in the market. Brands like RØDE that include products like RØDE Pod Mic, RØDE Caster Pro, and Focusrite 2i2 are good brands for beginners. Then, there are top tier brands like Universal Audio for Apollo interfaces, and others in that same tier level, like Neumann, Sennheiser, etc. Since there are many brands in the market, be sure to do your research to find the microphone that best meets your brand and budget.

With that being said, I will reiterate: you can begin a career in voice acting by simply using the equipment at your disposal.

Remember, you have to build up and level up. Rest assured that you will be able to find work as a beginner.

EQUIPMENT OPTIONS:

MICROPHONES BRANDS
- RØDE
- Neumann
- Sennheiser
- Sony
- Warm Audio
- Audio Technica

HEADSETS (PREFERABLY CLOSED)
- Sennheiser
- Beyerdynamic
- Sony
- Focal

INTERFACES
- Focusrite
- AVID
- RØDE Caster Pro
- Universal Audio-Apollo Twin or Solo

RECORDING DEVICES
- MacBook
- Mac Mini
- Tablet
- Personal Computers (PCs)
- Mobile Devices

RECORDING SOFTWARE
- GarageBand
- Izotope Rx Series
- Twisted Wave
- Audacity
- Pro Tools
- Studio One
- Source-Connect (to connect with client's studios)

FIND MORE INFORMATION REGARDING EQUIPMENT, VISIT:
- SweetWater.com
- GuitarCenter.com
- bhphotovideo.com
- zZounds.com

So, you may be wondering, where do I start? Well, there are many opportunities throughout the world.
In my case, I learned about the voice over industry through a friend.

After the discovery, I began my voice acting career by finding work on Pay-to-Play (P2P) websites such as voices.com, voices123.com, and castvoices.com. I will provide a reference list of other websites at the end of this book.

* Find more categories on page #114.

In the voice acting industry, there are a few ways to go about finding work. Some may prefer the old school route of finding work by utilizing agents, networking and marketing. The modern method is using Pay-to-Plays, or you may choose to join the gig economy through websites such as Fiverr and Upwork. You need to assess your preferences and working ability to determine which avenue works best for you. In the process, be aware that there are going to be pay discrepancies between the different paths. You may and most likely will do a mixture of both to gain the experience you need to continue to advance in the field.

Outside of booking work, there are other ways for you to build your voice acting portfolio. You can start by creating content on your computer, phone, or tablet. Posting the content you create can open other doors that auditioning may not reach.

To begin building your content, you record
your voice narrating public scripts or
mimicking shows you've watched.

Fortunately, finding scripts online is fairly easy, and there are a plethora of scripts from which you can choose. The key is to practice, practice, practice!

Networking with other voice actors is a great way to acquaint yourself with the profession. You can find online communities through Facebook groups, Pay-to-Play websites, YouTube, Instagram or online forums. The key is for you to immerse yourself in the field so you can better understand the local, national, and international voice actor market.

There are several pathways to seek employment for example Pay-to-Plays, Agencies/Agents, Gig Platforms, and Self Marketing Outreach. Remember, whichever path you choose, you will encounter many learning curves.

There is no one-path-fits-all. The key is to find that category of voice over acting that best fits your brand and style.

Some of the different categories in which your voice may shine includes: Promotion, Commercial, Audible Description, Political, Audio Book Narration, Dubbing, Movie Trailer, Anime, Character, Video Game and more. Oh man, the list goes on!

After some self-reflection and researching, you will begin to understand what you need to do to find work in the area best suited for you. This discovery may lead you to Pay-to-Play or gig economy websites. Also, you may choose to seek an agent or agency.

Work experience not only gets you paid, but it also helps you build your portfolio, which is imperative for you to develop your skills for better opportunities. You can also use your new-found earnings to purchase better equipment, hire a voice over coach or even get a new Voice Over demo. Of course, you can simply enjoy your earnings, but I believe that reinvesting in your craft is a must if you want to keep advancing in the profession. You will find a platform or method that helps you thrive.

* Find more categories on page #115.

While the voice acting industry is an exciting and even fun one, do not be mistaken, it requires persistence and diligence.

Conducting research on the voice over market is important because it helps you learn more about the different agencies and the expectations they have of their voice actors.

During your research and personal assessment stage, ask yourself this question: "In which space do I best showcase my voice?"

The key to answering this question could be as simple as determining the area in which you get the most bookings. If you are still a novice, you can also research creative content designers, creative directors, videographers, and engineers in search of voice actors. Your search can be as narrow as locally or city-wide, or as broad as state and nationwide. The more you're willing to hustle, the better the opportunities you'll encounter.

*Scan this for a video of 101 Voice Over Sites.

AUDITIONING TECHNIQUE TIPS

Don't just follow the script, embrace it!
It's easy to say follow the script, but you got to be the script too.

At the beginning of this book, I mentioned that your unique voice is an asset in the field of voice acting. The audition stage is your chance to sell your uniqueness, while also meeting the client's needs. Showcasing who you are as a person helps you standout.

Being a voice over actor requires that you understand the healthy balance between following your client's guidelines and conveying their intended messages and embodying the essence of the script.

Before your audition, research your client to understand their brand. This could come in the form of finding previous commercials or advertisements on social media or other platforms they utilize to showcase their brand.

Once you determine how they promote their brand, follow that roadmap in the format of 1-3 takes. A "take" is when you record the script they provide and "takes" are recording multiple recordings of the script on that mp3/wav file usually making sure each sounds different to show range and creativity. You may try three different takes incorporating styles they've utilized in the past.

Typically, I do a take of what they seem to want, then I tweak that version a bit before finally putting my own spin. Because I know how to improv, I am able to add my own technique to a script to give it a different flavor or style.

A good voice actor keeps up-to-date on the current trends of the industry.
In the past, the industry trend for a lot of commercial spots, for example, leaned towards cheesy, high-energy voice acting, but currently, the industry leans towards a more calm, cool, and casual tone, with a little emotion sprinkled in between every now and then.

To assess which direction the client intends to go with the script, it's best to first read the script and then ask questions that will help you better understand how to proceed. The dialogue created between the director and the voice actor helps build a relationship as well, due to sometimes you don't often see them in studio sessions.

CLASSES,
COACHING,
CONFERENCES,
AND
CONSISTENCY

Reinvest, reinvest, reinvest. Did I mention reinvest?

For continued growth in the field of voice over acting, you should be willing to put whatever you're earning back into your craft. I recommend that you invest in not just your equipment, but also the skill set. Your physical and mental well-being is also important.

You have to understand that this is a career. This is an industry. This is work. Just like athletes go to the gym every day, you have to go to your voice over gym daily.

Part of your voice over workout routine should include taking voice acting classes. These classes are integral to your success and to you expanding your network. Through taking the classes, you will begin to hone in on your skills, gain new perspectives, and create your support group of other voice over actors.

There are plenty of avenues through which you can take classes, and the costs also vary. Some popular websites include groundlings. com, realvoicela.com, acting.skillshub.life and globalvoiceacademy.com.

As you take these classes, make sure that you are applying the skills you learn to your craft.

It is also important to know that the knowledge you acquire through these classes may not always be useful, depending on your own individual circumstances. Even so, you would still be left with the value of having tried something new and gained a new perspective. While not immediately applicable, this knowledge could be to your benefit in the future. Along the same vein, if you want more of a personal feel, you can see if the class instructors offer coaching services as well.

Investing in coaching classes is a great way for you to get one-on-one time, which can be very helpful if you are looking to correct a specific issue or build upon your voice over acting techniques. You can also find a coach by conducting a search of your favorite voice actors, directors or producers. You may be surprised that they offer coaching services. Don't be shy, go ahead and sign up! Keep in mind it is okay to take a class or coach here and there, but you may see better results from consistently taking classes or receiving coaching sessions for 3-12 months straight.

Attending conferences is another way to grow in the voice over industry. Before you decide to attend a conference, make sure you have a plan.

You should know who you hope to see, who you'd like to meet or add to your network, the classes you'd like to take, and how those classes will help you advance your career as a voice actor.
Some conferences you can explore include VO Atlanta, ONE Voice, and That's Voiceover! Career Expo by Society of Voice Arts and Sciences (SOVAS). I will provide a bigger list at the end of this book.

Attending these conferences is a good way to build your brand. Your presence helps others in the industry know who you are and your genre of voice over acting. Once you establish your brand, it's imperative that it stays consistent. If you're establishing yourself as a commercial voice over actor, ensure that your professional websites and accounts showcase your work in this arena. While you can also showcase other skills, such as audiobook narration, make sure your commercial voice over work is highlighted in all the mediums you use to promote your work.

In addition to your professional skill set, your personality is a core part of building your brand. Show people that you are a stand-up, genuine person.

Your reputation will go a long way in this industry, so ensure that you build a good rapport with your clients by showing them that you are hardworking and reliable.

To achieve this, ask yourself the following questions when working with a client: Do I have fun and easy sessions? Do I create a positive work environment? Am I easy to work with? Do I take feedback and direction well? Am I able to efficiently complete the work? Do the people I am working with hold me to a high regard? Am I a great human?

With that being said, don't be discouraged if your session is not going as seamlessly as you'd like. When I did my first national spot (voice over commercial), just a few months after starting my voice acting career, I did around 100 takes with the client during that session.

During my second year, however, I was able to do the same script in just 50 takes. By then, I had built my confidence and developed the skill set I needed to embrace the script and make it my own. My professional growth made for a very successful experience with the client! The same audio engineer was there and provided me kudos as well!!!

As you start making money you might be tempted to not be as motivated about developing your skill set. I urge you not to fall victim to this trap. You have to continue to work to develop your craft. Consistency is key!

Every voice actor needs to have demos of their work.

While professionally-made demos are nice, they are not required (some may say otherwise). With the right amount of skill, you can create your own demo. At the beginning of my career, I hired someone to write the script I used for my demo, but I produced my demo, thanks to my background in making music. Beware that many seasoned voice actors would not recommend that you self-produce your demo.

I found producing my own demo to be affordable because I was able to find royalty-free music or beat instrumentals from YouTube Music to add as background to my vocal audio recording. I self-edited the entire project. In the end, this self-made demo was beneficial to my career as a voice actor.

As I've said before, only you can determine what works best for you. Even if you do not have a professionally-made demo at the start of your career, with a quality demo, you can start generating momentum, a clientele, and money.

Once you have the resources, you can inquire into companies that produce demos. I recorded my demo through Real Voice LA. Also, research seasoned voice actors to find out where they've gone for their demo production. You can generally obtain this information from their website either through them sharing it, or a notice stating their sponsorship through a demo/media production company.

I recommend that your demo reflect the genre of work you're seeking. For example, if your genre of choice is voicing movie trailers, this should be reflected in your demo.

Make sure that your demo showcases your talent, as it will set the tone of the quality of work you can provide. Also, make sure that your skills are on full display within the first minute of the demo, that way, you catch the client's attention at the very beginning. Your goal should be to make your prospective clients see and hear you as someone who can benefit their company.

You need to start thinking about how people can access you!

Gone are the days where you could rely on newspaper, radio, and television ads to showcase your voice over talent.

In this day and age, you need to start building your online presence through your own website and your social media platforms. You also need to start networking. Some examples include reaching out to creative directors, designers, and local media.

When you build your website, make sure it is easily accessible. An easy way to accomplish this is by having a simple website name. A good website also showcases a headshot picture and your current demo mp3. Your potential client should be able to easily listen to and download your demo from your website. This is critical because they can save your demo for reference or put you in their roster for potential work in the future.

Not sure how to structure your website? I can give you some inspiration through a walk-through of my website, BertoTheVO.com.

The main page of my website features my playable/downloadable demos, headshots, my biography, contact information, the top gigs/spots I've booked. Then, the next page displays my portfolio, where you can access a lot of the other work I've booked or been a part of. Be strategic about what you share on your website because it is often the first impression a potential client will have of you.

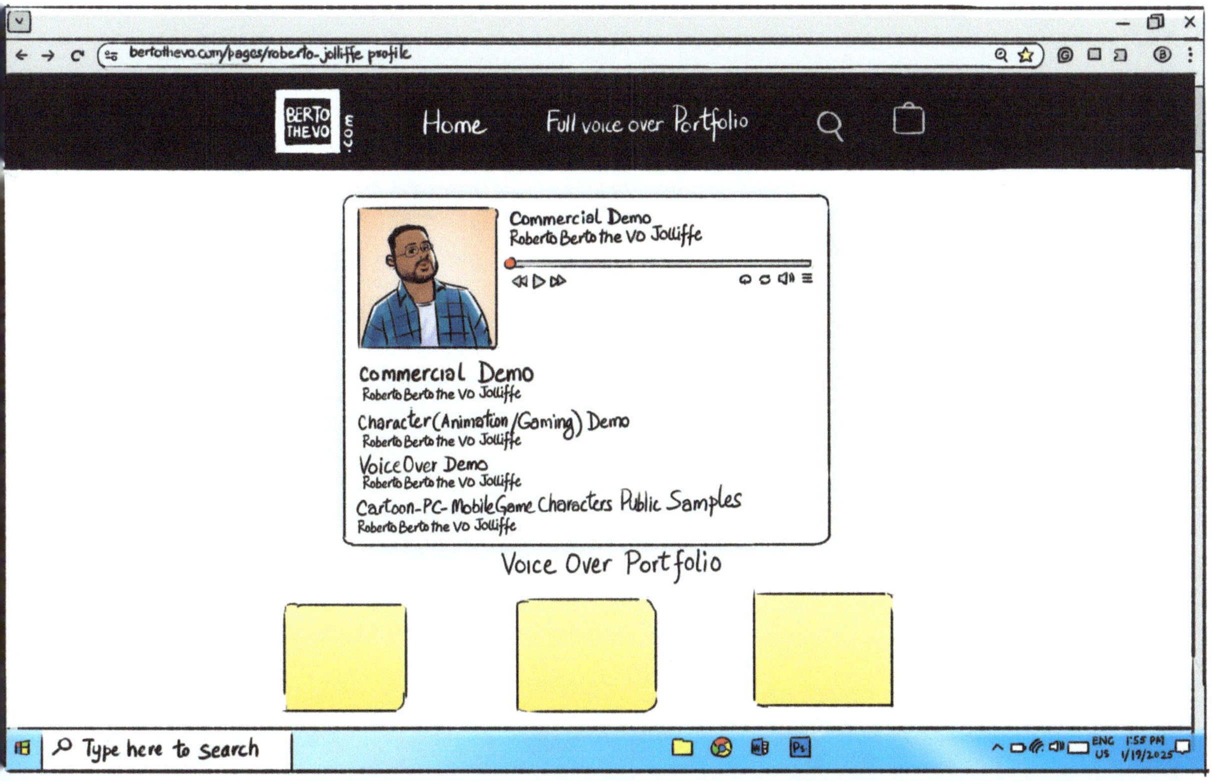
bertothevo.com/pages/roberto-jolliffe profile
BERTO THE VO .com
Home
Full voice over Portfolio
Commercial Demo
Roberto Berto the VO Jolliffe
Commercial Demo
Roberto Berto the VO Jolliffe
Character (Animation/Gaming) Demo
Roberto Berto the VO Jolliffe
Voice Over Demo
Roberto Berto the VO Jolliffe
Cartoon-PC-Mobile Game Characters Public Samples
Roberto Berto the VO Jolliffe
Voice Over Portfolio
Type here to search
ENG US
1:55 PM
1/19/2025

BERTO THE VO .com
Home
Full voice over Portfolio
Life
McDonald's
JUST DO IT.
LIQUID IV
vivid seats
THE Co-op
Mtn Dew
vivo
GRANDE CHEESE COMPANY
VIA
G
VISA
harri
NASCAR
DEPARTMENT OF THE TREASURY

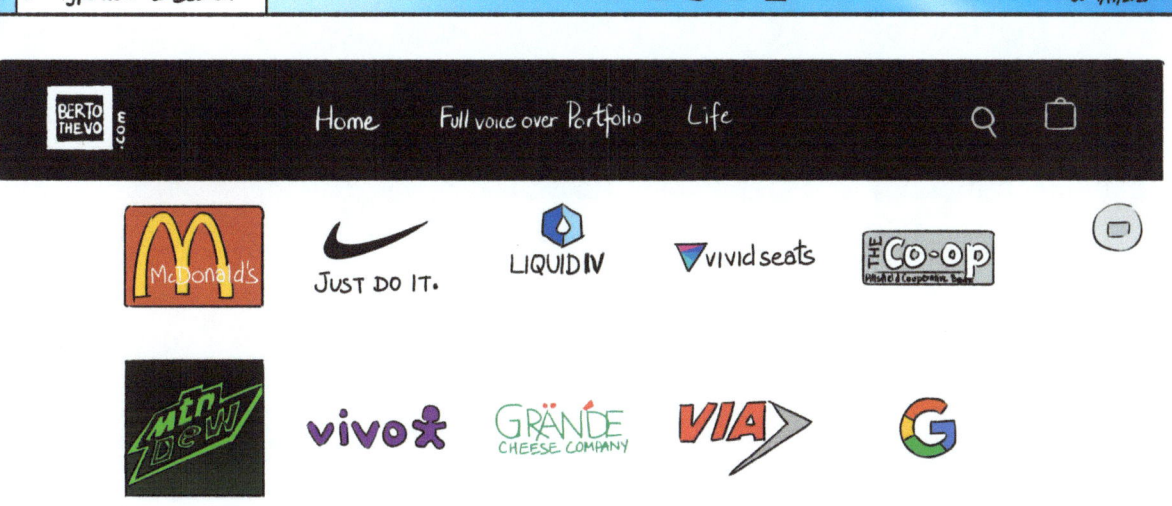

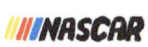

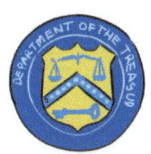

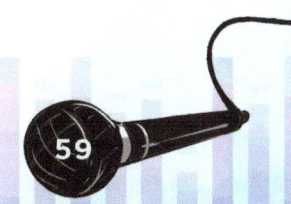

Although the purpose of this website is to book voice over work, it's good to include some information about who you are as a person. My page gives you a brief history about who I am. It lets viewers know that I am a Hispanic Afro Latino from Texas, and my parents are from New York (Nuyorican) and Panama. Viewers also learn where I grew up, and the jobs I've had. This background information not only gives a preview of my character and personality, but it also shows that I'm a versatile person. Being relatable can help open up future voice acting opportunities.

On your quest to find great voice acting opportunities, don't limit your experience to just voice over work. You can also showcase your talents through vlogging, reporting, radio, podcasting, gaming and most recently streaming.

MARKETING,
SEO,
AND BRAND
CONSISTENCY

You establish your brand through your website and your social media pages.

Be sure to regularly update your contact information on your social media pages and website, and also to keep the information and visuals consistent. You want potential clients to know it's YOU when they land on one of your platforms.

*Check out My Website BertoTheVO.com here to get examples.

Likewise, also keep your hashtags and handles consistent on all platforms. Your email should also be consistent as well as your social media handles, and I encourage that you use custom signatures at the end of your email.

Also, work on the SEO (Search Engine Optimization) of your website. Search Engine Optimization is the process of improving the quality and quantity of website traffic to a website or a web page from search engines like Google, Bing, or Yahoo. When potential clients are looking for specific voice actors in your genre you can become top choice with the right tags and website optimization. They can't book you if they don't see you!

By working on your SEO, you can curate the information that potential clients may see once they search information related to you as a brand.

As you determine what tags and hashtags to associate with your brand, make sure that they are all consistent. For example, if you're developing your brand as a particular type of voice over actor, make sure that those tags consistently display that skill set. You want potential clients to feel like they know you when they see you.

Marketing is also key. You have to learn how to market yourself. To showcase your skills, make business cards, and create reels or content that reenacts already produced content. Also, reach out to potential clients or leads. You can utilize tools like Nimble and other Customer Relationship Management (CRM) and lead generation tools.

These are two methods you can use to reach out to new clients not accessible on the Pay-to-Play websites or at the auditions that your agent books. The great thing about these tools is that if done right, you can create a process that helps you identify and reach out to new potential clients. It displays details from the background of the client, when you initiated contact, the last time you followed up and if you have actually made contact with the client. These metrics help you A/B test your email tactics so you can adjust to get engagement. Sometimes your emails get lost in the shuffle and if you have a system that can remind you when you should reach back out that can make the difference of acquiring a new client relationship. Remember you can email clients for years but the moment they say "Stop Emailing Them" please do so, it is rude and not professional otherwise.

You still have to hustle. You still have to get out there and make the moves because if you don't move your feet, you won't eat!

You have to figure out ways to reach other audiences or potential clients and look for keywords or key names that you work with or hope to work with in the future. For example: creative directors, creative production, audio assistants. There are a plethora of lists out there that you could utilize to start doing your email campaigns and bringing in different clients or exploring different markets. You have to step outside the box to get more money in your box.

P.S If you don't have time to do this or need extra assistance, hiring a VA or Virtual Assistance is also great for handling this task. You can find great ones at: www.vaforvo.com

Voice over acting is an art form. The best artists are constantly thinking outside the box to find ways to sharpen their skills. Studying real commercials, television programs, and people watching are great and simple ways to pick out new ideas to develop your skill set.

You elevate your art when you are able to mimic different speaking styles and voice inflections you are exposed to on a daily basis.

As I mentioned earlier in this book, there are a variety of classes, seminars, and conferences you can attend as you work on your skill set. You have the option of choosing in-person, online, live streamed, and pre-recorded events and courses.

You should also consider taking improv, acting classes, learning how to work with different audio interface equipment, microphones, headphones, and audio engineering programs or digital audio workstations (DAWs).

The key is to improve all areas of your craft. Refine your voice acting skills, learn how to better market yourself, increase your brand visibility and brand outreach, manage your contracts, and scale your career for higher earnings. During the course of your profession, dedicate time to work on these areas.

You should know that auditions also count as practice. So, audition, audition, audition! Auditions that don't require you to sign nondisclosure agreements (NDA's), are a gold mine for future reference, so keep that content.

You could run into a situation where you have a client who has a specific request for a voice over actor, like say a basketball hype man voice. If they don't have a script, you can choose from material from a past audition, and provide the sample that you feel works for what the client is looking for.

You want to make sure that you can provide versatility, readiness, and showcase the big toolset you have in your vocal arsenal!

As it is with life, you're going to have more losses than wins in this line of work.

The number of auditions you have will be greater than the number of bookings you get.

Keep your chin up, and don't let these minor setbacks get you down. It is also okay to get excited when you book a job. You deserve it! You can also celebrate when you're able to snag a big audition.

Also, remember, when you're presented with an opportunity, give it your all so that when you send that recording off, you know you gave it all you had.

Even when you miss the mark on a job, an audition can be a doorway to unexpected opportunities. Keep bringing your A-game; you never know who might be watching or listening and impressed by your performance.

For all you know, a producer might not like you for a particular spot, but may have another role more suitable for you.

Wins and losses are a part of life, but the key is to use them to propel your future success. Perhaps a loss will provide you insight on how to better sell yourself or develop your voice acting.

Mastery and success in voice over acting is a journey, not a sprint. Don't worry too much about your wins and losses. The point is to keep working to build your portfolio and perfect your craft.

Mastering every aspect of your field is crucial. In voice over, understanding the business is key. It's the compass for navigating talks with clients, sorting usage rights, and sealing deals with flair. Get savvy not just locally, but globally.

Stay on top of your business by tracking and recording your work and earnings, because at times, agencies may not have great tracking systems. You are responsible for knowing when you will receive your payments and making sure that your taxes are properly filed. Also, document your expenses. This includes money spent on equipment, educational content, travel, conference attendance, dining, and other expenses that help you expand your business.

Trust me, the more work you book, the more imperative it becomes to have a functional tracking system. I personally use a spreadsheet to keep track of my work, earnings, and expenses. This saves me the hassle of having to search through emails, texts, P2P platforms, etc. to obtain the information.

When contracting for work, you may be able to customize your payout method. For example, you can choose to be paid every 30, 60, or 90 days. Or in some cases you may be contracted to only receive payments after the project goes live.

Also, as you book work, be sure to document the different aspects of the job. Document when you performed the job, what the job entailed, what you were paid, and when you should follow up with the client if you haven't received full payment.

Recordkeeping also helps with goal setting. Make note of the marks you are or are not hitting, and how you can utilize the garnered information to scale your talent. You should know that this industry can be tricky. To avoid any pitfalls, it is also important that you understand the ins and outs of the business.

I suggest you chat with peers, communicate with important figures in the industry, and attend seminars to acquire more insight on the industry. I'll talk more about this later in the book.

PERPETUAL,
LOCAL,
REGIONAL,
NATIONAL AND
INTERNATIONAL
BROADCASTING

Various methods exist for determining fair pay in the industry, but thorough research is essential. Much of it is based on perspectives or what people believe you should be earning and industry standard.

You do have access to rate sheets through companies such as Global Voice Acting Academy (GVAA) and Voices.com. Because these worksheets cover rates for artists in different countries, make sure you use the pay rates customized for your area.

Rates can vary depending on specific job factors, such as amount of work, where the content will be shown and for how long. This includes considering local, regional, national, and international broadcast rights. Additionally, the airing length, whether it's for 2 weeks, 6 months, a year, or perpetuity, also influences the rates.

Many industry professionals seek perpetuity, but it's crucial to approach this cautiously. Ensure you don't inadvertently negotiate away your rights, including beyond perpetuity, such as in relation to artificial intelligence (AI), which is a significant topic in today's landscape.

*Scan this to view the GVAA Rate Guide.

Stay mindful of your contracts because this could impact your rate. Also, don't be afraid to follow-up with clients especially if you see a potential for contract renewals since sometimes artists' information may not be automated in their systems. For example, I've had a few contract renewals with Pop Tarts. If your contracts have the potential for renewal, ensure you follow up, especially if you're not automated in their system, to ensure fair treatment.

Want to ensure you don't leave any crumbs on the table when it comes to compensation? Well, the key is to study, study, study.
Stay informed about all aspects of the business and explore platforms like Fiverr, Voice123, and Voices. These Pay-to-Play platforms offer diverse compensation strategies. (which many in the industry may not agree with, but I want to make sure you are educated on all avenues)
In this field, you'll work with clients from various backgrounds, each with unique expectations. These platforms help you navigate client interactions and develop business skills beyond the platform.

Be prepared to handle direct inquiries via email, recognizing key indicators of client intentions. Experiment with different negotiation tactics, like probing for a budget before providing your rate, to potentially increase profitability.

Your pay for the work you receive may vary based on your work status, which can be influenced by your location (e.g., California, New York, Florida) and right to work states like Texas. Options include SAG-AFTRA, SAG-E (eligible), Union, Non-Union, and Fi-Core.

Working Actors can utilize Unions in the entertainment industry to help negotiate contracts, get the right pay or rates, and get health care. Once a working actor completes a job, they are unemployed until they land the next role or opportunity. Most people think they are paid in between jobs, but no, oftentimes, voice actors have to budget until the next job. A benefit of becoming a Union actor is that, while the amount and period of payment may vary based on contract terms, these actors typically receive residuals for their work. Non-Union actors, however, do not. Additionally, many of these Unions provide equity and help actors establish the foundation necessary to build a reputable career in an extremely competitive, ever-changing industry.

As is the case with all things, stop over thinking and give it a try! You may come across jobs on casting platforms but feel that you're not an exact match for what you have to have to offer. Don't let that discourage you from auditioning.

When I first started, I auditioned for everything because I wanted to get some notches on my belt. Trying out different roles (even if they are not a "fit") can help you determine your skill level, so you know what to improve.

If you never explore other voice over genres, you won't discover your strengths or weaknesses. Trying different genres and taking courses can clarify if it's a path you want to pursue. It's better to learn sooner rather than later. With 8 billion people in the world, there's bound to be someone who appreciates your voice. Have fun experimenting and pushing your limits. In your recording booth, it's just you against the world sometimes.

My advice to you is: record and put your voice to use. Once your audition is submitted, let it go. Avoid overthinking or comparing yourself to others. Everyone starts somewhere, and success takes time. Focus on your journey, improve, and have fun trying new things.

Trying new things is part of the fun in voice acting. Do not box yourself into a specific genre because you might be able to get more clients and showcase your broad spectrum of versatility if you open up your mind to different categories.

You may never truly know what category of voice acting is or is not a good fit for you until you actually try them out.

I once wanted to be a regular actor until I attended an in-person acting class. Witnessing someone effortlessly recite a script in a different accent within a week amazed me. It made me realize there's so much more to acting than I thought. Testing my limits helped me understand my capability. But I would have not known what my limits are if I had not tested my limits.

In the field of voice acting, it is important that you expand your personal horizons and knowledge. Retain what resonates with you. Recognize your strengths and comfort zones. Stay open to new experiences, like my venture into improv.

You're going to try things, but it's not always going to feel right. Trust me, with time, you'll understand what feels right. Directors appreciate actors who take risks, try new things, and offer different interpretations. Remember, one bold move can distinguish you from the crowd. Keep pushing forward because the extra effort pays off when you're ahead of the pack.

Look, the future, climates, and technology are constantly changing, especially in today's world. I advise you to embrace change.

AI discussions are common, especially regarding perpetuity contracts and voice re-creation usage involving AI-generated voices. Ensure you understand your voice rights and explore how to leverage technology for your benefit rather than fearing its potential drawbacks.

We have a chance to shape the future, carve our own paths, and use technology to enhance our work. While it can be intimidating as technology advances, we should also view it as an opportunity for growth.

Instead of dwelling on the challenges that change may bring, embrace change, adapt, and discover ways to stand out in a sea of uncertainty. Your focus should be on pivoting to new opportunities and evolving your workflow.

Currently, organizations like National Association of Voice Actors (NAVA), Screen Actors Guild (SAG), Writers Guild of America (WGA) are fighting for our rights as creatives. NAVA has a great AI Rider on their website for you to reference and utilize in contracts. Keep an eye on organizations like these to stay informed and find ways to support the future of the voice over industry.

Roberto V. Jolliffe III is a multi-hyphenated individual with a passion for creative pursuits, encompassing art, music, technology, DIY projects, and business endeavors. As a Panamanian and Puerto Rican raised in a military family, his diverse experiences and perspectives have shaped his worldview. His career in the technology and innovation sector has provided him with the opportunity to develop innovative applications and engage in entrepreneurial activities. Traveling extensively has allowed him to immerse himself in various cultures, enriching his understanding of the world.

Reading is a cornerstone of his intellectual journey, particularly biographies, origin stories, mannerisms, and captivating narratives. His insatiable curiosity, historical fascination, and willingness to experiment and take risks have guided him to his current position in the Voice Over Industry. From class clown to talent show host, rap song creator, morning radio show intern, acting classes in Texas, improv classes at Groundlings in LA, and starting a podcast before pivoting to Voice Over mid-pandemic, all involved voice in some way. Each experience has honed his voice-related skills and provided valuable insights into the industry. This book aims to be a pivot that leads to new career paths, a learning experience that can be applied to future endeavors. It presents the techniques and industry acumen needed to explore the Voice Over field, making it accessible to people from young children to adults.

Driven by the belief that this knowledge can serve as a pivotal catalyst for personal growth and career advancement, Jolliffe authored this book. His intention is to illuminate the behind-the-scenes aspects of a Voice Over talent. He's not saying these are the only steps to success, but rather sharing techniques and industry knowledge to help others improve their journey. Presented in an engaging and visually appealing illustrative format, the book aims to captivate readers of all ages and backgrounds, fostering a new and exciting approach to learning and exploration.

My goal was to write a book that was appealing to people of all age groups, and detailed enough to provide a thorough guide to those interested in entering the voice over industry.

Special thanks to my WHOLE family and MYSELF for the continued support and inspiration to complete this book. I want to give a major shout out to the team at Bird House Publishing for bringing an idea I had in my head to life, couldn't have done this without y'all!

I hope you enjoyed this read, and I'd love to learn how this book has helped you start your journey as a voice over actor. My contact information is on my websites at BertoTheVO.com , TheVOBook.com, email: RobertoJolliffe@gmail.com and social media @BertoBoushae so get in touch! Last but not least, welcome to the wonderful and vast world of voice over acting!

Respectfully,

–Roberto

The Beginning...

I would like to thank you, Aunt Jay, for letting me stay at your house for 6 months in LA in 2019, while I began this journey in the arts and entertainment industry! I gained so much more than education. During my stay, we connected and pushed each other on a spiritual level. Shout out my boy Will Brown who told me about Voice Over work while I was in LA.

His tip started me on this journey. Shoutout to the person who read books to my brother and I every night after work and made us read out loud (It helps with my scripts now) my Moms, Delilah Santiago, and my wife, Stacy Jolliffe, for always supporting me on this journey and all the crazy ideas and passion projects I have tried from childhood to adulthood! I would also like to thank my Pops, Roberto Jolliffe Jr. for giving me a passion for music, bass lol and living life on my own terms. My brother, Javiel "Jay-Q" Jolliffe, for always hearing me out and letting be me no matter how much he didn't like it lol.

Mike Williams who has been on the ride with me from my young adult years in San Antonio until now, what a time lol. Also, I have a lot of close friends who always pushed me to be great. For example, Roderick Burke, who I've known since middle school, traveled the world and bucked the system with , Maurice "MoTown" Redrick, who has always showed me that I can do and be more, Marshall Felder for always working with me on any wild ideas I have, Sam Cook, for hearing my potential when I came back from LA and began the podcast journey, with Maverick "Mav P 365" Pascal and I, who went on his artistic creation journey in his own right at the same time as I did. Mav, it's always been good sharing that energy with you and building our futures together!

-Berto

This book is dedicated to my kids and nephews (future nieces too): Jacey, Khali, Beaux, IV, and Jayton! Y'all can do anything you want in this world, all you have to do is be passionate, work hard, stay consistent, and dream bigger than anyone can imagine! Remember, nobody can be or think like you!

Love Daddy/Uncle Bert

APPENDIX/ REFERENCES

MICROPHONES BRANDS
- RØDE
- Neumann
- Sennheiser
- Sony
- Warm Audio
- Audio Technica

HEADSETS (PREFERABLY CLOSED)
- Sennheiser
- Beyerdynamic
- Sony
- Focal

INTERFACES
- Focusrite
- AVID
- RØDE Caster Pro
- Universal Audio-Apollo Twin or Solo

RECORDING DEVICES
- MacBook
- Mac Mini
- Tablet
- Personal Computers (PCs)
- Mobile Devices

RECORDING SOFTWARE
- GarageBand
  - Izotope Rx Series
    - Twisted Wave
      - Audacity
- Pro Tools
- Studio One

Source-Connect (to connect with client's studios) Find more information regarding equipment, visit:
- SweetWater.com
- GuitarCenter.com
- bhphotovideo.com
- zZounds.com

STUDIO BOOTHS
StudioBricks
Whisper Room
Vocal Booth To Go (for traveling)

PAY TO PLAY (P2P) PLATFORMS
- Voice123.com
- Voices.com
- CastVoice.com
- VoPlanet.com
- Voquent.com
- Bunnystudios.com

For more information regarding P2P websites, visit: Top 101 Voice Over Websites- https://www.youtube.com/

GIG WEBSITES
- Fiverr.com
- UpWork.com

AGENCY LIST
- Atlas
- ACM
- CESD
- PB Talent - Pastorini-Bosby Talent
- Wehmann
- BigMouth
- SBV Talent
- DPN
- DDO - Dorothy Day Otis Agency

CONFERENCES
- VO Atlanta
- One Voice Conference US/UK
- That's So Voice Over (SOVAS)
- eVOcation
- Mid Atlantic Voice over (maVO)
- WonderCon
- PAXeast
- Euro VO Retreat
- National Association of Broadcasters (NAB)

SCRIPT SITES:
- myactorguide.com
- Voiceactorwebsites.com/free-voice-over-scripts/
- Edgestudio.com/script-library
- Voice123.com/blog

VOICE OVER CATEGORIES
- Promotion (Promo),
- Commercial,
- Audible Description,
- Political,
- Audio Book,
- Dubbing
- Audio Drama
- Narration,
- Movie Trailer,
- Anime,
- Character,
- Voice Matching
- Live Announcer
- Radio
- Foley
- Video Game
- International Categories (other Languages)
- Mobile APP
- Corporate/Explainer
- Telephony/IVR
- E-Learning
- Sensual
- Meditation
- Audio Engineering
- Producer
- Radio Imaging
- Streamer / Streaming
- Spoken Word
- Toys
- Website

LEAD GENERATION OUTREACH CATEGORIES

TYPES OF INDUSTRIES TO LOOK AT:
- Broadcast

Media
- Computer Games
- Entertainment
- Marketing and Advertising
- Media Production
- Motion Pictures and Film

JOB TITLES TO LOOK FOR:
- Casting Director
- Associate Producer
- Booker
- Casting Agent
- Casting Assistant
- Casting Associate
- Casting Booker
- Casting Coordinator
- Casting Intern
- Casting Producer
- Casting Professional
- Content Producer
- Creative Consultant
- Creative Director
- Creative Executive
- Creative Head
- Creative Lead
- Creative Manager
- Creative Producer
- Creative Services
- Segment Producer

AUDIO/VIDEO PRODUCTION SPECIALISTS
- Executive Producer
- Media Producer
- Production Manager
- Senior Creative
- Senior Producer
- Talent Agent
- Vice President Creative
- Video Production Manager
- Video Production

VOICE OVER SPECIALISTS
- Voice casting
- Voice manager
- Voice over agent
- Voice over director

SCREEN ACTORS GUILD (SAG UNION), NON-UNION AND FI-CORE:

SAG/UNION:

When people say they are a SAG actor it is the same as saying they are a Union Actor. This is a membership-based Union which typically cost $3,000 to join and where you pay yearly/ quarterly fees to support the Union. This exists in other countries as well; for example, ACTRA in Canada and Equity in the United Kingdom.

The Union representation typically means that the actors are considered more skilled, more tenured, and overall, more professional than their Non-Union counterparts. This gives you an advantage in the search for clients. Also, once you attain this status you can no longer work Non-Union jobs, which will limit the amount and type of work you can do. The good thing with the Union is that your pay structure is well-defined and contracts around them are pretty standard across the board.

In this status, monies from the work you book will pour into your retirement pension and healthcare benefits. You will be entitled to residuals for certain bodies of work you do that continually live on after a specified usage period. This also requires the producer to do more detailed documentation to the Union on what the project is, its location, budget, etc.

NON-UNION:

So now that you have an understanding of a Union actor, let me breakdown what a Non-Union actor is. A Non-Union actor is not a member of the Union. Non-Union actors range from people who have limited experience to veterans in the field. That being said, along with no barrier to entry, the talent pool is bigger than the Union and the range of professionalism could vary widely.

Pay structure is out the window when it comes to Non-Union compared to Union. Some people could over work you and not pay you your worth or you could be subject to minimal payment amounts that Unions would find inadequate. Non-Union actors are not held to any standards in regard to the jobs they can or can't work. You also do not receive residuals once you work your job, unless you are renewed. Renewals typically only happen within a specified time frame in your contract.

Non-Union actors are considered SAG-E or SAG Eligible when they work a number of jobs that are defined as Union jobs. In this case, after performing a Union job (depending on the state) you will be Taft Hartley'd (taken from the Taft-Hartley Act) which gives you a window of 30 days to work a Non-Union job. Then after that, you have to convert over to Union jobs.

FI-CORE:

Fi-Core, also known as Financial Core, is a designation in the industry that some say "walks the line." It allows Union actors to denounce their status, but they are still able to work Union jobs while also picking up Non-Union jobs. However, they cannot publicly identify themselves as SAG-AFTRA actors. Instead, they put "Fi-Core" on their resumes or out in the public so it is clear what jobs they can work. This can affect the Union jobs they are auditioning for. While an actor may choose the side of the Union they stand with, this designation in particular brings on judgement from the entertainment industry. When choosing this designation, be sure to think through the effects this can have on your career.